Joseph Campbell's

Hero with a Thousand Faces

BookCaps™ Study Guide

www.bookcaps.com

Table of Contents

Historical Context

Joseph Campbell was born in White Plains, New York in 1904. While growing up his parents took him to cultural places such as the Museum of Natural History in New York City and Campbell became very interested in Native American History. He spent a lot of time learning about Native American society and was especially intrigued by Native American mythology. After Campbell graduated from the Canterbury School in New Milford, Connecticut he received his B.A. in English Literature from Columbia University and his M.A. in Medieval Literature.

Before completing his graduate degree Campbell traveled to Europe with his family with permission to study abroad for a semester. In Europe Campbell became greatly interested in, and subsequently influenced by, theorists such as Carl Jung and Sigmund Freud, and writer James Joyce. He also influenced and gained influence from a couple of well-known men who were great friends of his: John Steinbeck and Hans Zimmer.

While Campbell was responsible for writing many non-fiction pieces concerning mythology and theory, *The Hero with a Thousand Faces* is perhaps one of his best known and influenced George Lucas in the creation of *Star Wars*. For *Hero with a Thousand Faces* Campbell used the work of Jung, Freud, and Arnold Van Gennep to develop his own model of the "hero" in literature.

The journey of the hero is referred to as the "monomyth", a term which he borrowed from James Joyce's *Finnegan's Wake*. Campbell's basic idea is that there is a fundamental structure and progression in all mythology throughout the world, regardless of the place of origin or time period: the hero ventures from his everyday world to a world that is supernatural, he fights and beats the forces there, and he returns home to share his tale with others. Campbell's monomyth has been received, accepted by, and served as influence for many literary and cinematic minds since its revelation in 1946.

Plot

"Hero with a Thousand Faces" is Joseph Campbell's explanation of the world of mythology and the journey of the Hero. Campbell relates mythology to Freudian and Jungian concepts of the subconscious, though he admits that the notion of mythology, culture, time, space, and spirituality are transcendent amongst cultures and yet remain to be interpreted in varying ways. Campbell describes the journey of the Hero as a means to explore the essential truths of what it means to be human and what the responsibilities of a human should be. Campbell explores the duality of everything in life; the mother and the father, the universe and the individual, but mainly the physical and the spiritual world. According to Campbell the Hero experiences a change which inspires or forces him to go on a journey searching for truth. Along the way, he encounters a supernatural being which will offer him protection and guidance. On the journey, the Hero will encounter many obstacles and challenges though they will be less severe if he is respectful to those individuals he meets along the way.

Once the Hero has reached his destination he will gain much knowledge and truth of the world and be responsible for delivering this knowledge to his people, though they may not be receptive. Upon returning, the Hero will eventually be greeted with death and reborn to begin the cycle again. According to Campbell, this is the journey that all must take, though it manifests itself differently dependent on the culture.

Themes

The Journey

The theme of the journey is representative of the journey that individuals take throughout life, the journey to a spiritual awakening, the journey toward knowledge and enlightenment, and also the journey of the universe. The mythology of the journey stretches to many different cultures, religions, and societies, and, in each one, the journey is manifested differently. While the journey is interpreted different for everyone the language of the journey, represented with symbolism, is a concept that is universal.

Duality

The concept of duality is central to Campbell's notion of the Hero's journey. According to Campbell there is duality in every aspect of life which alludes to all things being one and the same. For every representation in the world, there is another representation which is both opposite and equal. For example, Campbell uses the mother as the good and nurturing force while the father is the tyrant. He also uses the example that God is separate from all things yet He is also in all things. The duality is also reflected in the cosmogonic cycle of the individual, as well as the cycle of the universe as a whole.

Spirituality

Spirituality is something which is largely present in mythology. The concept of the spiritual being remains vague in most myths because the story must be universal to transcend various cultures and belief systems, but the idea of a higher power is always present. The Hero is on a journey for spiritual enlightenment and truth that he can deliver to his people, which gives the Hero a godlike power that the everyday man may not be receptive to. This is in modern day religion as well; man can be on a spiritual journey and search for meaning and truth though not all men would agree with what is learned.

Responsibility

In undertaking the journey the Hero is taking the responsibility of attaining a knowledge and enlightenment that not every man possesses. In undertaking this task, the Hero is responsible for spreading the wisdom and teaching others the knowledge which he has acquired. Though the Hero has the option to use his knowledge for evil and tyranny, he can choose to go the responsible route and head back to a place where he may not want to be because he knows that it is his duty to pass on what he knows. He feels as though it is his responsibility to repay those who have supported and protected him.

Creation

The concept and question of creation is addressed in several sections throughout this book. There are varying ideas throughout the world's religions on how the world came to be and how mankind was formed, though all seem to have something to do with a virgin birth and the idea of Immaculate Conception. According to Campbell, all individuals, and the Earth itself, exist on a cycle which plays out and restarts as needed. The man who is born from the virgin birth is part god and thus when he dies he will return to the virgin womb and be born again.

Universality

Universality is something which is very important in mythology because while all myths seem to follow the same outline. The specifics are not necessarily the same, so symbols must be used to represent the characters. Universally, the world was created, and a hero was born. The hero goes on a journey, achieves enlightenment, brings the knowledge back to his people, he dies, and he is born again to keep the cycle going. The earth also eventually reverts back to its original state and begins again. The overall concept is universal, though the specific language may not transcend.

Symbolism

Symbolism is the vehicle used to relay the message of the journey in mythology. Because different cultures, religions, societies, etc. have varying languages and specific stories of creation, spiritual beliefs, and values symbols must be used as universal representations. For example, to Christians the virgin birth and subsequent journey described would identify most closely with that of Jesus. For other cultures, it may represent the journey of another god or spirit. The symbol of the World Navel is used to represent any significant point of truth and beginning, dependent on the culture.

The Female

The female in the context of the Hero's journey is representative of comfort and protection. Generally when the female is mentioned it is in reference to her womb, which is the source of comfort and protection for the unborn child. When the Hero begins on his journey he is greeted by a supernatural force which offers him protection and guidance along the way and this being is generally manifested in the form of a female, as well. The female can also be represented negatively but always in duality with a more positive purpose.

The Cycle of Life

The journey is essentially the cycle of life, or as Campbell calls it the cosmogonic cycle. The man-hero is born of virgin birth, he seeks enlightenment and thus takes a journey to find it, he overcomes the obstacles that stand in his way, he discovers his father and thus enlightenment, and he accepts responsibility for taking his knowledge home and sharing it with others. After sharing the knowledge, the hero dies, enters non-existence, and replants within the mother's womb to begin the process again. Similarly, the earth will run its course until it must revert to its original pre-creation form.

Perseverance

Perseverance is one of the defining characteristics of the Hero. He sets off on his journey and he never gives up, even when confronted with challenges that the mortal man may not be able to overcome. He sticks true to his journey and his goal and does not waver even when tempted with appealing alternatives, such as living a new life in a new place or accepting unexpected power. The Hero knows what is expected of him and what he is responsible for, even if it is unappreciated by others. He knows that he will be rewarded for his good deeds by the powers that be.

Chapter Summaries

Prologue

This book was published for the first time in the late 1940's. The author, Joseph Campbell, is a mythologist who is thought by some to be a philosopher. He uses the typical scenario of the hero's journey in literature to explore the nature of human actions and truths and also to develop theories, themes, and purpose of duality, symbolism, and universality between literature and reality.

The Prologue consists of the sections "The Monomyth", "Myth and Dream", "Tragedy and Comedy", "The Hero and the God", and "The World Navel". Beginning with the section called "The Monomyth" Campbell explores the idea of myth within the realm of humanity; through culture, experiences, and society.

Campbell supports the idea of the unconscious and the work of Sigmund Freud and Carl Jung, which he often uses to describe the human relationship with myth. People experience things in different ways through different cultures but the experiences come together within the subconscious is what creates the very basics of human nature and truth. Campbell suggests that dreams and myths are interchangeable and are influential of one another. For example, a dream that a man had in which he killed his father and then took care of his mother is representative of the Oedipus myth.

Many actions, such as that of Oedipus, are grounded in our subconscious desires which are part of the Hero's journey. Every society has rituals which are manifested from subconsciously motivated or mythically-oriented belief systems. Campbell also points out that some archetypes appear in dreams which involve a journey, a set of obstacles, and the aid of an elder along the way. This is the same journey the Hero must take, with the purpose of bringing his newfound wisdom back to his people. In the section called "Tragedy and Comedy," Campbell suggests that tragedy and comedy are both equal parts of life. He notes that, while humanity has an affinity for happy endings, death is the only real ending to life, and it results in the void of non-existence. Campbell states that tragedy is the sad pain of realizing the ultimate truth of life, while comedy is the ability to find joy alongside that pain. In terms of the journey and the circle of life, the comedy, or joy, of life is that even when it ends it is not over but will begin the cycle once again. In "The Hero and the God," Campbell surmises that, after the Hero's journey, he has gifts of knowledge to bestow upon his fellow man, which makes him godlike. He received the aid and protection of the supernatural along the way and was introduced to his father, a god, which made him realize his own godliness.

"The World Navel" is the place within all of mythology which serves as the central point; it is the center of the world and the point from which all truth is born. The World Navel can be a place which affirms life, or it can be the place which destroys life. In some myths, the World Navel may be a mountain, a tree, or a point of religious representation. For example, the activities of Muslims revolve around Mecca. Everything in the world emerges from the World Navel and thus it deserves the utmost respect.

Part One – Chapter One

Part One is the "Journey of the Hero". This chapter consists of five sections called "The Call to Adventure", "Refusal of the Call", "Supernatural Aid", "The Crossing of the First Threshold", and "The Belly of the Whale". "The Call to Adventure" is often the first stage of the hero's journey in myths and fairytales which is the beginning of a big change, often by accident. Sometimes the decision to change and the circumstance which leads to it are deliberate. After the change, the Herald is introduced, which is the character that announces the beginning of the journey.

The third stage is the introduction of the setting which often represents the subconscious which the Hero will soon explore. Campbell suggests that these character types appear in many short stories and fables and often follow a similar journey and encounter many treasures as well as dangers. In "Refusal of the Call" the Hero will refuse the adventure at first and become imprisoned, be it physically or psychologically. They do not refuse the call forever; only until they have a psycho-spiritual moment which follows by a spiritual intervention that pushes them forward into their adventure. "Supernatural Aid" occurs after the Hero has refused the call and a supernatural presence intervenes. This presence will offer spiritual aid, wisdom, knowledge, and support and is representative of destiny.

The presence is gifted supernaturally and is able and often willing to provide both guidance and protection to the Hero on his journey. The character of the "Supernatural Aid" is often female and is manifested thusly, such as the Virgin Mary or Mother Nature. It is likely that the figure is a woman because it represents nurture, the power of protection and destiny, and the peacefulness of a paradise atmosphere, as the mother's womb.

In "The Crossing of the First Threshold" the Hero will first enter into a physical world that it outside of the Hero's home village and which represents the hero's understanding of their self and soul. This is when the Hero is confronted by a Guardian, which is a dangerous presence sent to test the Hero's resolve to move forward.

The adventure that the Hero is on is always a passage into the unknown where they must deal with unforeseen dangers and choose whether to continue on. The Hero must defeat the Guardian using both physical abilities and psychological ones such as persistence. The Guardian is generally impressed by determination and thus allows the Hero to pass through.

The next stage is "The Belly of the Whale" in which the Hero is swallowed either psychologically or physically and must use determination to fight his way out of the belly of the beast. The Hero must draw all of his courage and see his personal truths to move forward from, essentially, a spiritual death. Many characters who are swallowed either physically or metaphorically find themselves in a new physical world inside of their own subconscious.

Part One – Chapter Two

This chapter consists of "The Road of Trials", "The Meeting with the Goddess", "Woman as the Temptress", "Atonement with the Father", "Apotheosis", and "The Ultimate Boon". In "The Road of Trials" the Hero finds himself confronted with many challenges, both physical and psychological, that he must overcome to continue on his journey. Along the way, he meets spiritual guides, which may help him on his journey, though they may not. The guides are a means of reminding the Hero who he really is, to keep him humbled, and to remind him of what his purpose is.

Next is "The Meeting with the Goddess" when the Hero meets a woman who is all things; beautiful, ugly, life-giving, life-destroying, generous, and violent. The woman represents all of the things that can be possible in life. At this time, the Hero will either be respectful or disrespectful; if he is respectful he will be rewarded and if he is disrespectful he will be punished. In some cases, the goddess will tempt the Hero to sin, which is the subject of "Woman as a Temptress".

Campbell believes that society as a whole is too concentrated on intolerance and sin, especially when it comes to male/female relationships, when it can be more beneficial to work toward psycho-cultural awareness.

In "Atonement of the Father" Campbell suggests that the image of God is an archetype of the father and of a source of power. In order for the Hero to assume this source of power, he must come to terms with the image of his father and to become that image. It is thought that the father represents for a male the symbol of what he will be become and for the female the image of what her husband will be. Becoming one with the father is equal to accepting one's world and their place in it.

The Hero must embrace the father in order to achieve enlightenment. The next step is "Apotheosis" which deal with duality; the idea that opposite characteristics can come together to form a whole. There is an acceptance of androgyny, which must be achieved, and an acceptance of the dual concepts of the Ogre-Father and Goddess-Mother, as explored in previous stories. There is not a difference between the concepts of transcendence and life because one leads to another thus they are the same.

The goal of the journey that the Hero is on is to unite dual concepts. "The Ultimate Boon" is the ultimate goal of the Hero's journey, which is a connection to what is eternal. "The Ultimate Boon" is the gift awarded to the Hero after overcoming struggles on his journey and striving forward. Campbell believes that the Boon is something that mankind is always striving toward, if not selfishly, because it is something they crave even though that craving is rarely quenched.

Part One – Chapter Three

This section explores "Refusal of the Return", "The Magic Flight", "Rescue from Without", "The Crossing of the Return Threshold", "Master of the Two Worlds", and "Freedom to Live". By "Refusal of the Return" the Hero has accomplished many things. He has rescued the female, he has retrieved a source of power, and he has achieved the enlightenment that he has sought for a long time. After a journey of such magnitude, it is now time to return home, but the Hero does not want to because, if he does, then he is responsible for sharing with others what he has learned. In many cases, the Hero does return home, but sometimes he does not; sometimes he decides to stay at the place he has arrived, knowing it as a place of happiness and accomplishment. "The Magic Flight" is what the Hero goes through when he does decide to return home.

There are two different journeys that the Hero can make; the first journey is under the protection of the goddess if he has earned her protection, and the other and more common journey is when the Hero has had to defeat and go against the wishes of a powerful being to achieve his goals. If the Hero is on the latter path, he will encounter many obstacles on his return journey, often more than he encountered on the first half. In this case, the Hero can create obstacles for his pursuers to overcome if they are to catch him; much like the physical or psychological obstacles he had to overcome himself.

In "Rescue from Without" the Hero is unable to get away from the place he has arrived in accomplishing his goal and he must be rescued. The person who rescues the Hero is likely to be an ally that he has left behind or a person who is loyal to the god or goddess who is protecting him. The Hero subconsciously realizes that there is a life to be lived in the place he is trying to return to and thus he must get there at all costs.

"The Crossing of the Return Threshold" deals with the Hero's journey home. Campbell poses a question of why the Hero would want to return home, where he would have to share his wisdom and teach what he has learned to others who will not likely believe him. The simple answer is because it is necessary for him to return. People are often caught up in their day to day lives and at times need to be reminded that there are greater powers at play, and there are many things going on that are not seen but are distinguished.

It is the Hero's job to teach these things to the people he left behind to remind them that there is something greater in the world. Only a true Hero would strive to accomplish the goal of teaching, even if he did not particularly want to do so.

The Hero must embrace his knowledge and power and share it whenever possible, even if no one wants to listen. In "Master of Two Worlds" Campbell explains that sometimes the Hero has internalized his knowledge and power to the point that he is able to pass between the two worlds which he knows, as a reward for his hard work. Though this passing between worlds may not be literal, it is spiritually and symbolically important and relevant.

At this point, the Hero no longer needs to strive but to relax and allow what may come. "Freedom to Live" appears to be the Hero's freedom to live as he chooses as a reward for his work. The Hero now realizes the world he has always known is only an illusion and now that he has lived a life of freedom and adventure he is truly able to live freely, without ties to a false reality.

Part One – Chapter Four

This section is called "The Keys". Campbell begins by summarizing the Hero's journey thus far. The Hero has explored different areas of purpose, suffered complications and hardships, and has taken in the support of various supernatural powers. Campbell also makes it clear that myths are not to be taken at face value because over time myths evolve to conform to the thoughts of that time and their meanings become more or less relevant depending on the person who is listening. He cautions taking myths too seriously because sometimes the symbolism is dropped and the stories, characters, circumstances, etc. are taken too literally.

Campbell points out that this has happened with Christianity and the stories in the Bible. He believes that the way many of the stories are perceived now is a secondary interpretation, rather than the initial proposed meaning. Campbell does not allude that the stories of the Bible are interpreted falsely, but that mythology must be interpreted in every way possible before the true meaning can be represented and inferred.

Part Two – Chapter One

Part Two is the "Cosmogonic Cycle". The sections discussed within this chapter are "From Psychology to Metaphysics", "The Universal Round", "Out of the Void – Space", "Within Space – Life", "The Breaking of the One into the Manifold", and "Folk Stories of Creation". In "From Psychology to Metaphysics" Campbell explores one the main themes of his theory, which is the relationship between psychology and mythology.

According to the work of Sigmund Freud and Carl Jung, amongst other psychoanalysts, the evidence of a relationship between psychology and mythology appears to be pretty conclusive. In terms of dream analysis, the path of the Hero and the logic of mythology and fairy tales seem to follow the same structure of the dream. Campbell does not, however, believe that myths can be directly correlated to dreams because dreams do actually have the potential to be affected by the life of the dreamer.

Dreams tend to come from the everyday experiences and real life of the individual dreamer, while myths come from the experiences of humanity as a whole. Just like in the Hero's journey, humanity emerges, survives, and returns to what it emerged from, which is the process that Campbell refers to as the "Cosmogonic Cycle". The places the Hero emerges from and returns to will be different for different cultures, which is why language is too limiting; because of the limits of language symbols are used which are endless in their possibilities and are universal.

The union of symbols and myth is representative of the Hero's journey toward discovering that union; it is duality. "The Universal Round" is the term that Campbell gives to the three-part cycle of life and the Hero's journal; he emerges, he lives, he returns. According to Campbell this cycle mimics the cycle of the waking experience, the dreaming experience, and the dreamless/deep sleep experience. The cycle continues, and unity is achieved; all is one and one is all. While everyone may have a different experience, universally the cycle is the same.

In "Out of the Void – Space" Campbell discusses the explanations that various cultures and religions create for the emergence of life. Each society and culture, and especially religion, has created its own explanation for creation and the process of life coming out of nothingness. There are many stories and myths about how God created the world and how He gained power. Each society has stories which support the creation of their world; a world which suddenly emerged from nothing.

These myths explain how the basic elements of the world were created such as wind, fire, metals, air, and the concepts of day and night. "Within Space – Life" explains how people were placed on the Earth, in terms of the myths which come from various cultures. While the stories may be different, the symbols and ideas follow the same basic structure. The structure includes the creation of male and female and the unity of the egg and seed which together create life, as a form of spiritual unity and duality.

The unification of the egg and seed into life is the basic building block upon which the rest of the physical world has been created. "The Breaking of the One into the Manifold" is where Campbell discusses the emergence of One once he is created and his journey. The journey after emergence can take an easy, blessed, graced, or tense road, but it will always lead to enlightenment if the journeyman perseveres.

The realm between safety and freedom is a place a person can live, but it may involve struggle. This is another example of duality; another example of this duality is the way God is in all things but He is also separate from all things. In terms of this journey and of life, it is lived with struggle but also in the light of God's peace.

In "Folk Stories of Creation" Campbell touches on the folklore that each culture has regarding the creation of the world. The stories all seem like anecdotes with no sincerity to them or no search for deeper meaning. He notes that the folktales he has heard make no attempt to search for the larger spiritual meaning behind the various theories of existence.

Part Two – Chapter Two

This chapter consists of sections titled "The Virgin Birth – Mother Universe", "Matrix of Destiny", "Womb of Redemption", and "Folk Stories of Virgin Motherhood". In the first section, Campbell so eloquently states that the "world-generating spirit of the father" (semen) comes into the earth and the experience of life by passing into "a transforming medium – the mother of the world" (the womb). This basically means that the semen of the father is the life impulse which grows in the womb of the mother which is a place of nurturing. The mother is a virgin because the father who impregnates her is the "Invisible Unknown". Campbell quotes this idea from a book of Finnish myths which recounts a story in which the mother, or the sea, gives birth to all things including a god after being "impregnated" by an unknown source.

In the "Matrix of Destiny" Campbell discusses the mother and that idea that the mother is a "universal goddess" in most cultures and myths as she takes on many forms. The mother represents duality within herself; she can bring life or take it away, she can be a virgin and a harlot all at once, and she can be a monster or a queen.

The universal goddess becomes the "Matrix of Destiny" in that she alone contains the truth of each being's destiny, which presents itself in her various manifestations.

The "Womb of Redemption" pertains to the virgin birth. There are many immaculate conception stories through various cultures though perhaps the most well-known example is the birth of Jesus by the Virgin Mary. The child who is born of virgin birth serves as an example of a new awareness or a new consciousness for those surrounding him, as did (does) Jesus.

The virgin who becomes impregnated with these new being now holds a certain power herself as the life nurturer who has been chosen. At one point, Christian missionaries travelled through South America and found that the Aztecs had virgin birth stories of their own, which infuriated the missionaries as they though the Aztecs were deliberately making a perversion of the story of Jesus. Similarly, the goddess Parvati in Hindu mythology prepared herself to unite with the god Shiva which proved as another perversion on the story of Jesus' birth.

On the same token Campbell discusses "Folk Stories of Virgin Motherhood", similar to the previous "Folk Stories on Creation". There are many varying stories on virgin birth throughout different cultures, though all of them follow the same basic premise and theme, which in this case is virgin birth.

The difference between the stories is usually the manner in which the virgin womb was fertilized; there are many means of fertilization according to these stories thus it seems that there is a possibility to be reborn at any time and in any place. The fertilization does not always result in the birth of a hero or savior but can also result in the birth of a demon.

Part Two – Chapter Three

This chapter is called "Transformations of the Hero" and contains eight sections; "The Primordial Hero and the Human", "Childhood of the Human Hero", "The Hero as Warrior", "The Hero as Lover", "The Hero as Emperor and as Tyrant", "The Hero as World Redeemer", "The Hero as Saint", and "Departure of the Hero". In the first section, Campbell discusses the ever-evolving mythology of cultures as time goes by to adapt with the changing values and beliefs. At first, the spirit figures took the form of the father and the mother, but they evolved into the more relatable and humanistic figure of the Hero-Emperor and such counterparts. The main difference in this new Hero is that he became more man than god and taught others how to be more like him.

The things that this new Hero accomplished were things that happened in real life. For example, there is a legend involving a Chinese Emperor who worked on a farm, studied mathematics and science, and married a woman who discovered the process for making silk. Despite being born supernaturally, this Hero managed to live the life of a normal man.

In "Childhood of the Human Hero" Campbell discusses the differences between the god-hero in the first part of the book and the man-hero in the second part. The god-hero in part one took a psychological journey into the subconscious while the man-hero in part two has the task of united God and spirituality with human life. Both heroes must work to unite the physical and spiritual worlds, though they do so from opposite ends of the spectrum.

"The Hero as a Warrior" pertains to the role of the Hero in terms of his responsibility to his place of birth. The place where the Hero receives his wisdom is known as the World Navel and the wisdom which the Hero gathers from the World Navel it is his responsibility to impart on the people of his birth place. He becomes an incarnation of wisdom and must move past the negativity he had previously experienced in his life to bring a new freshness of life back to his home.

In "The Hero as Lover" Campbell likens the freedom that the Hero wins from his battles to a woman. In this regard, the Hero not only wins freedom, but he wins love, as well. This is essential because love is one of the spiritual goals of humanity and also serves as a union of the principles of male and female. Just as the Hero was tested on his worthiness, strength, and courage for freedom he is also tested on these same factors in regard to his union with a woman.

"The Hero as Emperor and as Tyrant" is in regards to the Hero's journey to learn the identity of his father.

The Hero does not know the identity of his father because, in this case, the father is the spirit which implanted the seed in his mother's virgin womb. The Hero asks for the identity of his father and is told, though, in some cases, the news causes corruption in the Hero. The Hero may then desire the tyrannical power of his father, and when this happens he only becomes what he has already defeated; the Hero has continued the cosmological cycle.

"The Hero as World Redeemer" is what happens after the Hero has learned the identity of his father. The man-hero will then return to his home acting as a prophet, or acting as the embodiment of his father with the notion that they are one and the same. The man-hero's duty now is to break the control of his tyrant father and unleash the spiritual power that the father holds.

The father is a dual entity, as are many other factors of Campbell's analysis, and is thus both a life-giver and life-taker. If the Hero is to break the cycle that would be continued by him becoming a tyrant as well, he must sacrifice the part of himself that holds the life-taking side of his father. This is the dichotomy which exists in the world; we must choose whether to give in to the demons or to prevail to goodness and the life of a Hero. "The Hero as a Saint" is the final way in which a hero may manifest himself. This occurs when the man-hero has been so profoundly affected by his spiritual awakening that he can no longer exist within the living world. When this happens, the Hero must withdraw himself from the world with the hopes that he will only continue to have a deeper understanding and relationship with his own spiritual nature. "The Departure of the Hero" is the Hero's final journey which is into death. This is when the man-hero comes full circle and is once again within the realm of all that is spiritual. The man-hero must embrace and accept death as an inevitable and illuminating part of the life experience.

Part Two – Chapter Four

This chapter is titled "Dissolutions" and contains two sections; "End of the Microcosm" and "End of the Macrocosm". Within this chapter, there is a discussion of the way death is represented in mythology; both the death of the individual and the death of the universe which are inevitable parts of the cosmogonic cycle. In "End of the Microcosm," the man-hero views death as a way to reconnect with the Unmoved Mover (i.e.: God, the Great Spirit, etc.) Just like the original journey, the journey into death can have many obstacles and struggles. It can also be dangerous just as the Hero's journey to enlightenment. Death has always, in various cultures, been seen as a time of ritual and a time of prayer which may be because of the process. In death, according to the Ancient Egyptian Book of the Dead, body parts belonging to the Hero are fused with body parts of the gods, unifying the man-hero and the god into one. Similarly, the spirit of the deceased individual will become one with the spirit of the god.

After the spirits and body parts become one, they enter the cosmic egg where they are set to enter the cycle once again into life. "End of the Macrocosm" is a similar idea, only it deals with the end and subsequent rebirth of the universe as a whole, rather than the individual. Rather than fusing with the spirits and preparing for rebirth the universe reverts back to the state it was in when life came into being. When the physical life and universal life cycle as one they result in the ultimate union between individual and universe; or the physical and spiritual worlds.

Epilogue

The Epilogue consists of four sections called "Myth and Society", "The Shape-shifter", "The Function of Myth, Cult, and Meditation", and "The Hero Today". In the section, "Myth and Society," Campbell explores the relationship between myths and the societies which they come from. Each culture has its own beliefs and its own truths, which result in the birth of myths. There are many different relationships between myths and the societies, cultures, or religions from which they sprouted though the common thread seems to be that they offer knowledge of that culture in some way.

The way myths are interpreted is explored in "The Shape-shifter". Campbell maintains that there is no set means of interpreting myths, nor is there any set meaning or manifestations that can be taken from each myth. The interpretation of the myth is up to the individual who is consideration said myth. Campbell gives psychologists and philosophers as an example; they all view things from a wide range of influences and sources though none of these differences are seen as wrong, but rather they are all valid in their own way. Interpretation has no right or wrong.

The section "The Function of Myth, Cult, and Meditation" deals with perception. Campbell suggests that there are many characteristics which a person "wears" in their everyday life as though a piece of clothing; for example: gender, career, nationality, appearance. According to Campbell these various layers of "clothing" are only things that we wear while functioning on this particular plane of existence which is our everyday lives. Spirituality is a way to strip ourselves of this clothing and connect with a higher level of being and different cultures have myths and rituals which help them to do so, and which help them to embrace the idea of a cosmogonic cycle.

The spiritual goal of most is not to see the world but to realize that they are a part of the world and have the freedom to wander around that world both physically and psychologically. Again in terms of duality, the essence of an individual and the essence of the world are one and the same. In "The Hero Today" Campbell explores the notion of the Hero and his journey toward enlightenment and spirituality within today's society.

Campbell believes that humanity as a whole has become entirely too materialistic to bother with the thought of anything outside of the physical world. They seem to have forgotten about the mystery in the universe and instead have become consumed by what immediately surrounds them, even the activities which seem trivial, desperate, or artificial. What humans today do not realize is that the "monsters" they deal with in everyday life (financial institutions, politics, religion, science, etc.) are all representative of the monsters that the heroes of myth face on their journeys. Campbell makes the suggestion that every person in today's society has a responsibility to his/herself to become a hero and make the hero's journey. They should overcome obstacles, obtain enlightenment, and share this new knowledge with others in the hopes of continuing the cycle and allowing society to thrive and to succeed.

About BookCaps

We all need refreshers every now and then. Whether you are a student trying to cram for that big final, or someone just trying to understand a book more, BookCaps can help. We are a small, but growing company, and are adding titles every month.

Visit www.bookcaps.com to see more of our books, or contact us with any questions.

Cover image © kmiragaya - Fotolia.com

Printed in Great Britain
by Amazon.co.uk, Ltd.,
Marston Gate.